Before You Begin...

Would your colleagues describe you as a leader or executive that is able to inspire and influence your people into achieving outcomes?

Would you like to have a way to assess your effectiveness in understanding your own mindset and harnessing this knowledge to then successfully engage with multiple stakeholder groups and lead change within your business?

We're here to help.

Over the past 19 years at Sloan Group International we've helped thousands of executives and managers just like you to develop the skills, capabilities, and strengths required to succeed as a boss, a contributor, and as a leader.

This brief volume will teach you the four dimensions of Executive Presence, provide tips and exercises to expand on your strengths and develop areas that challenge you, and give you a new level of confidence in your ability to succeed.

This book is designed as a useful introduction to the core concepts of Executive Presence. For more information about our Executive Presence & Influence programs and to take our Executive Presence assessment visit us online at www.sloangroupinternational.com.

ISBN: 978-1-0878-5950-7

TABLE OF CONTENTS

INTRODUCTION

The ability to instill trust and confidence in your people, even during times of disruption or discontent is an invaluable skill in business. How do we do that as leaders and managers? Through something called Executive Presence.

When we think of Executive Presence we often think of leaders who command a room, who have a certain ineffable quality that gets people to follow them. We often think of those with Executive Presence as great speakers with a strong personality, but what is it really? What enables one leader to grab people's attention and get them to take action when others can't?

After witnessing the world's most powerful leaders for many years, that "certain something" has become clear - it's a powerful combination of four types of presence:

- ☆ Somatic Presence (physical voice, pace, tone, tenor, posture, and coherence)
- ☆ Emotional Presence (grabbing an audience through authentic emotional connection)
- ☆ Mental Presence (structuring and forming your communication rationally)
- ☆ Charismatic Presence (telling compelling stories, and instilling a sense of confidence, trust, and power in those around you)

Executive Presence might be something you were born with - something natural and easy for you that comes from deep within. For most of us it's not innate, it's something that's carefully honed and developed over time. It is important to note that Executive Presence is a skill, not a trait, which makes it teachable and means it is something that you can learn.

Executive Presence requires us to understand and use our own mindset, coupled with the confidence to apply a range of communication methods that best enable people to see, hear and understand you, and for you to be able to do the same for them.
Great leaders make other people feel heard, understood, and inspired to take action. That's real Executive Presence.

Executive Presence is what distinguishes you from other leaders; it is what empowers you to influence those around you into actioning real change or outcomes in an environment that may even be negatively geared in allowing you to do so. The organizational structures of companies are becoming increasingly matrixed, as opposed to the traditional hierarchical approach, highlighting the need for more effective leaders as they can no longer rely solely on positional authority to influence change. Executive presence, and the skillset it is comprised of, is often an overlooked aspect of being an effective leader. It is not about being the loudest person in the room, but rather the person with the presence that enables them to communicate both verbally and nonverbally and empowers them to convey confidence and trust, particularly in times of uncertainty and change.

Have you ever had a leader that is able to command the attention of everyone in the room as soon as they enter it? A colleague that is able to achieve outcomes from people that were viewed as difficult to motivate or manage? A leader with Executive Presence is able to gain people's trust and willingness to follow by not only the way they present themselves but also by the way they are able to understand how they are perceived by others.

I work with a gifted leader and manager named Kathy Hamburger. She's been the CEO of multiple companies and people who've worked with her would follow her to the ends of the earth. When you listen to the qualities that make her so beloved by her teams she is a textbook example of a person with Executive Presence. A petite blonde with a hearty laugh, Kathy knows how to read a room and how to engage any audience easily by making them feel comfortable and by owning her authority. Kathy commands respect based not on her many accomplishments, those give her credibility but it's not what she leads with. Kathy commands respect because of her deep belief in her people to achieve great things. They can feel it, hear it, see it in her actions and words and they want to prove her right. When she gives them a vision of what's possible, they know it's real.

If we break it down, Kathy connects emotionally with her audience, she gives them a sense of confidence and optimism through the strength and confidence of her convictions and the power of her pace, tone, and body language. She tells stories that engage her audience and that serve a purpose to deliver a message, and she takes the time to structure her message so that it flows naturally and people can follow. She also repeats that message enough times and in enough ways that she engages people with different styles and gets them to remember what's most important.

Now Kathy is not the tallest, most commanding, most dominant or imposing leader that we may think of when we think Executive Presence. When we think of the media versions of leadership we might not think of a small blonde with endless energy, eternal optimism and engaging stories - that's because we forget that real Executive Presence isn't about the way we look, it's about the way you make others feel! Kathy makes people feel confident, cared about, and like they want to make a positive impact and make her proud.

Executive Presence is comprised of four key components; Somatic, Mental, Emotional and Charismatic, each of which play a crucial role in a manager's ability to lead their team. These four competencies provide a simple, yet powerful and practical model for executives to identify which aspects of their presence need more focus. Additionally, the model helps leaders diagnose which competencies are needed most in a variety of high-stakes situations.

Benefits of Executive Presence for leaders include:

- The ability to "read a room" and adjust as needed to achieve presentation/meeting objectives
- The ability to focus on critical information when presenting, speak with confidence, clarity and relevance
- The ability to tell useful, powerful stories to augment discussion and deepen audience engagement
- The ability to respond to resistance with healthy debate instead of disempowered, confrontational reactivity
- The ability to expand self-awareness and awareness of others
- The ability to model exceptional leadership skills in any situation and enroll others including senior leaders in a vision regardless of preconceived objections

What The Research Says

☆ **EXECUTIVE PRESENCE CAUSES PEOPLE TO LISTEN:** A group of 34 leaders, consultants and HR professionals completed structured interviews in which they described people who have different forms of Executive Presence. They subsequently responded to a validation study that confirmed the major findings from the interview analysis. The results highlighted an important distinction between leadership and presence. Effective leadership causes people to act; effective Executive Presence causes people to listen.

☆ **EXECUTIVE BEHAVIOUR IMPACTS INNOVATION:** A study in Strategic Management Journal investigated the relationship between innovation and executive behaviors and influence versus social culture. Using survey data from six countries comprising of three social cultures, executive behaviors and influence were found to have a strong positive relationship with product, market and administrative innovations. In addition, executive behavior and influence impacted both types of innovation, while social culture only had impact in the case of administrative innovation.

☆ **EXECUTIVE PRESENCE IS MULTI DIMENSIONAL:** A study conducted by Gavin R. Dagley and Cadeyrn J. Gasking published in Consulting Psychology Journal sought to understand the meaning of Executive Presence. From interviews with 34 professionals, 5 main findings emerged:

1. Executive Presence is based on audience perceptions of the characteristics of particular people

2. 10 core characteristics affect Executive Presence (status and reputation, physical appearance, projected confidence, communication ability, engagement skills, interpersonal integrity, values-in-action, intellect and expertise, outcome delivery ability,

and coercive power use)

3. Perceptions are based on impressions made during initial contacts (first 5 characteristics) and on evaluations made over time (second 5 characteristics)
4. The characteristics combine in different ways to form four presence archetypes (positive presence, unexpected presence, unsustainable presence, and dark presence)

5. The majority of the executives described as having presence were men.
The findings serve to highlight the complexity of Executive Presence, particularly in terms of the breadth of characteristics that underpin this construct and the influence of unconscious bias on people's perceptions.
Sorry ladies, frustrating though it may be, that means we sometimes have to work harder and more consciously on the skills in this book!

☆ **EXECUTIVE PRESENCE IS IMPORTANT:** 2012 survey of 268 senior executives conducted by the Center for Talent Innovation determined that Executive Presence accounts for 26% of what it takes to be promoted into leadership positions. Being perceived as having leadership potential is key to being considered for (and promoted into) leadership roles, and this requires a baseline of self-confidence, self-awareness, and charisma that get one noticed in a positive way.

CHAPTER 1 – Somatic Presence

A strong confident person can rule the room with knowledge, personal style, attitude and great posture." - Cindy Ann Peterson

What is Somatic Presence?

Command of physical posture and gesture/verbal pace and tone.
Projecting your voice with confidence, awareness of posture and adapting your stance to meet the situation. Voice, face, body and words are congruent. Feeling physically energised when standing in front of a group or working one on one with someone.

Somatic Presence in Action

Somatic Presence is grounded in the physical body, and it's all about being clear and congruent. It requires us to match our voice, pace, tone, posture and message so that we are communicating one thing with no confusion.

In 1941 Professor Albert Mehrabian published a book on body language entitled "Silent Messages", reviewing his research into non-verbal communication. He combined the statistical results of the two studies and came up with the now famous—and slightly erroneous—rule that communication is only 7 percent verbal and 93 percent non-verbal. The non-verbal component was made up of tone of voice (38 percent) and body language (55 percent). Why is this not quite the right rule? It's because the original research behind it was on how one's body and tone of voice communicated the meaning of a single word. That's not quite research on communicating complex ideas. It is CLOSE to the truth though. We know that good communication is more than just a well reasoned argument constructed out of a combination of persuasive words. We know that in order to be persuasive, we can't be robotic, distracted, or have a different facial expression than is appropriate for the tone of the message we're giving.

Body language goes a long way. Whether we know it or not, we're always reading the cues and signs that show how someone is feeling about what they are saying. Are they confident? Are they reluctant? Are they questioning what they are saying? Much of this is given away by body language and vocal tone. When we're aware of our body language we can stop ourselves from communicating the wrong message.

Negative body language might include:

-folding your arms in front of your body in a protective stance

-tense or stoic facial expressions

-eyes downcast, not meeting the gaze of others

-sitting slumped with head pointed down

-fidgeting, doodling, or twitching

That negative body language can betray your own distraction, irritation, or disinterest. When we work to integrate our message with our body language and tone of voice we can truly invigorate our communication and get people to pay real attention.

Remember this- Executive Presence is about how you make others feel. Think of the best leaders and bosses you've ever experienced. How do they communicate with you? Do they shrink down into a ball during a conflict? Do they say one thing and do another? No way! Great leaders communicate not just with their words but with their voice, posture, tone, and even with their eyes. They look, sound, and feel like they care. They are authentically present in the moment instead of being distracted. They demonstrate confidence in their perspective and drive their points home through cohesive messages.

A Somatic Presence Case Study

Theresa, a very smart and capable technology executive was a stressed-out mess every time she had to present in front of her fellow executive team members. Instead of delivering her message in a confident and relaxed way (the way she would with the project team she managed), she would look down, speak in a quieter voice than usual, and would tap on her glasses unconsciously. To make matters worse, she was concerned that she was the only woman in an all-male executive team in Silicon Valley, and she felt like they dismissed what she said no matter how she said it. When she thought about it, she would avoid preparing her updates to the team until the last possible moment, because the whole exercise just seemed futile. After a particularly awful executive team meeting where she'd presented a fantastic update about being ahead of schedule and on budget for a major product launch and been virtually ignored by the rest of the team, she decided to take matters into her own hands and practice her Executive Presence by focusing on her pace, tone, and posture. In working with a coach she realized that she had been blaming her lack of success with the team on them, when there were techniques she could learn that could be valuable. The first thing she tried was using a more commanding posture and tone. Instead of sitting during her next team meeting, she would stand with her shoulders back and her feet planted and present her update with a series of three slides. She practiced using a louder tone than usual and centered her voice in her chest instead of her head. She might not be feeling super confident, but she sure would look like it! The experiment worked, and everyone on the team commended her for her performance in her next meeting.

Tips for Somatic Presence

When you want to appear confident here are a few useful tips for positive body language:

1.Relax and open your posture. Instead of folding arms and crossing legs, put your arms down with feet straight on the floor. If you are tall, make sure you don't have your hands on your hips which can be perceived as aggressive or overly dominant.

2.Use your eyes. Make eye contact and maintain it without staring. When we hold the gaze of another person for a few seconds at a time, it shows we are present and actively listening and connecting.

3.Avoid fidgeting. When people touch their face or fidget when answering questions they can be perceived as being dishonest or covering something up.

4.Nothing beats a smile. Smiling authentically is infectious, and people want to feel positivity and smiling is the easiest way to help others to feel accepted and relaxed. Don't force it, as a forced smile is equally off-putting!

CHAPTER 2 – Mental Presence

"Your results are influenced by the mental zone you choose to live in"- Keith Webb

What is Mental Presence?

Mental Presence is the ability to stay focused on the task at hand, regardless of outside factors, whilst still being adaptable and able to improvise. It includes structuring your communication rhetorically in order to persuade others through a well reasoned argument.

Mental Presence in Action

If you are mentally present as a business leader or manager you might display the following behaviors:

- You actively listen

- You stick with the core topic and bring the conversation back to the task at hand

- You flexibly approach conversations while remembering the objective of conversing

- You think through what you are communicating and how to do so effectively

- You use logic and ask others to give you logical arguments

- You let go of your own solutions and stay open to the input of others before announcing a decision

Mental Presence demands a balance between the ability to stay focused on the task at hand, regardless of outside factors, whilst still being adaptable and able to improvise. The highly demanding nature of the fast-paced business world can make it extremely hard to be able to prioritize tasks and stay focused. The fast-changing and increasingly dynamic climate of modern day business demands companies be agile and flexible in their approach to problem solving in real-time in order to achieve business objectives. The ability to be flexible and think on your feet when faced with changing circumstances is a key component of Mental Presence. The way to feel confident and capable of getting your message across and being flexible is simple - BE PREPARED by exercising your rhetoric muscles.

The ancient Greeks knew all about Mental Presence. 2000 years ago Aristotle said rhetoric was "the art of seeing the available means of persuasion." He focused on public speaking or oration and he carefully laid out how to create the most persuasive, most powerful speech. There are multiple types of rhetoric according to Aristotle: Judicial rhetoric (arguing the facts), Epideictic rhetoric (demonstrating something), or Deliberative rhetoric (painting a picture of the future). There won't be a test, but it's good to know where this wisdom comes from.

Rather than focusing on the past or the present, Deliberative rhetoric focuses on the future. It's the rhetoric of providing a vision of a positive or negative future - for example when an activist gives an impassioned speech about what will happen to the environment if we don't clean up our act and change our attitudes towards pollution, or when a politician paints a picture of a better society if they get your vote. The famous "I have a dream" speech from Martin Luther King Jr. is one of my favorite examples of Deliberative rhetoric. Many of us have his words indelibly etched into our memory, with the vision that "my four little children will one day live in a nation where they are not judged by the color of their skin but by the content of their character."

What makes for good Deliberative rhetoric? According to our 2000 year old friend Aristotle, it's three things:

1. Ethos
2. Logos
3. Pathos

These three things enable us to create a deliberate change of opinion, a deliberate commitment to action, or a deliberate decision through our powers of persuasion.

Ethos is how you convince an audience that you are trustworthy and credible. This can come from using your background and status, your charisma or charm, or even unspoken body language demonstrating your confidence. (Somatic Presence, anyone?)

Logos is how we use our logic and reason to structure sound persuasive speech. This can include using data, statistics, facts, analogies and examples. It's the structure and content of the speech itself, and effective Logos is clear and understandable. It means we set up a strong argument. Logos is all about Mental Presence!

The main dimension of the information, argumentation, and structure is a verbal one, thus the speaker has to express these categories as simply, clearly, and explicitly as possible that the audience can follow his reasoning.

The possibilities of the audience to grasp the argument are limited, hence the speaker must communicate in an understandable way. Additionally, the possibilities of the audience to critically analyze the argument is also limited, thus the ability to create an argument that appears sound is sufficient because rhetoric deals foremost with functionality not with correctness.

- Bernhardt Kast, European-Rehtoric.com

Pathos is the appeal to emotion. Pathos rallies people to emotional states. This can be a positive state, like our leader Kathy Hamburger who makes people feel optimistic and capable, or it can be negative. Think of the powerful beauty industry and the advertising directed at women to purchase products to make them more youthful, thinner, or prettier. The emotion they evoke in those ads is often that of fear, shame, or lack, and that set of negative emotions is a powerful driver to purchase products that might alleviate those negative feelings. Pathos will become more relevant when we get to our next chapter on Emotional Presence.

The key to effective rhetoric is to internalize those three elements and structure your communication accordingly. For those of us that need to get our message across, there's nothing better than thinking through these three areas together and coming up with a structured approach. Over time, we start to think this way naturally and integrate rhetoric into our communication on a regular basis unconsciously.

Case Study: Mental Presence

Lately Tim has been reflecting on his days at work and realizing he often feels as though he is sleepwalking through his days. Tim, normally an energetic salesperson and team leader, was feeling low and his enthusiasm for the team leadership role was waning after two quarters in a row not meeting his team sales quota. To top this off, his boss was asking him to get his team performance to improve drastically, OR ELSE. Tim realized that he needed to re-invigorate the team to meet their sales targets and it might require some preparation.

Instead of winging it on their weekly sales team call, Tim decided it was important to pitch his team the same way he would pitch a client. He knew the team trusted him, so he had to use his position to inspire them into action. In thinking through the logic of the situation, he started with a statement. "We've all been disappointed in our numbers this past quarter. None of us want a repeat and what we really want is to exceed our goal by the end of next month. In order to do that we need a reset. First, I know we have the best product out there. Second, I know I have the best sales team and that you all have the capability to get great results because I've seen you do it."

Then he thought about how to get the team emotionally engaged. He decided to have them each tell a story of a success they had in the past, and talk about why they had that success. He would point out the specific strengths of that person during each story.

Finally, he thought about what would be a powerful way to keep the team's energy up during crunch time. At the end of the call he would offer an incentive on a daily basis for the team. Instead of individual bonuses or incentives, he'd focus on team wins. He set a daily goal, and for each day they met or exceeded that goal they would put $20 in a jar toward an end of quarter celebration.

It may sound simple, but walking through the exercise made Tim's enthusiasm go up, and he was able to rally the sales team into exceeding their quarterly goal by the end of that coming month.

Tips and Exercises for Mental Presence

If you want to increase your mental presence as a business leader, you can do the following:

1. Discipline your mind:
Be willing to give your full attention to your team members. Choose to put all other things aside during the conversation. We have to learn to give our solutions for the team members and allow the team member to lead his way to discover his own.

2. Remove distractions:
For Mental Presence to thrive, leaders have to stay in an environment that will encourage you to focus. If you are using Skype, turn off your email and any social networking sites. We must learn to turn off our phone. Silent mode isn't good enough, very few people can resist looking at the phone when a text message notification appears.

3. Focus your mind before the conversation:
Show up and start being present 5 minutes before the conversation with a team member. We must learn to put aside our other work – physically and mentally.

4. Focus during the conversation:
One of the ways to help our Mental Presence is to let go of our own ideas, strategies, and solutions. We have to inculcate the attitude of listening carefully to our team members. Ask questions from different angles to increase perspective. Don't be formulaic. Risk asking questions that are not part of your 'plan.' Go with your intuition.

Mental Presence can take a lot of physical energy. It takes even more mental discipline. Let's get in shape.

Exercise: Structure Your Communication Like the Ancient Greeks!

When preparing for an important communication (it could be to a small group, an individual, or a large audience; anything will do) write down the answers to the following questions:

a. What will enable my audience to find me credible and trustworthy? How can I establish that trust quickly? (Ethos)

a. What is the logic behind my argument? Why should they change their behavior, performance, or listen to what I'm saying? What are the facts I can use to defend my point of view? Why is it important? (Logos)

a. How do I want my audience to feel? How can I pull at their heartstrings and get them to feel that way? (Pathos)

CHAPTER 3 - Emotional Presence

"I've learned that people will forget what you said, people will forget what you did, but people will never forget how you made them feel." – Maya Angelou

---

What is Emotional Presence?

Emotional Presence encompasses an individual's ability to help others to feel that they are important, acknowledged and paid attention to by focusing on them without distraction in all interactions – a crucial component in leading people. It is the extent to which a person can perceive the feelings of others easily, naturally ask questions and listen intently to them. A key component of Emotional Presence is also an individual's ability to control their emotional state through self-management.

Emotional Presence in Action

A key component of Emotional Presence is also an individual's ability to control their emotional state; projecting a positive outlook most of the time. This competency within Executive Presence is what distinguishes a business professional from a business *leader*. Business intelligence amongst executives is somewhat an expected or a given quality, however emotional intelligence and the impact it can have is an often overlooked aspect within business professionals. An individual that has spent time understanding and developing their own emotional intelligence becomes more effective and impactful within their role as they are able to harness that understanding to better communicate and influence the people around them.

Every organization wants an individual who has Executive Presence or has the potential to develop it. This is because there is a higher level of productivity when there is a high sense of leadership and purpose. Emotional Presence encompasses an individual's ability to have honest self reflection on how their behaviors impact staff and their resulting emotions in order to make more purposeful and result-driving actions.

Remember that rhetoric! Emotional Presence enables us to influence through Pathos - the emotional connection to what we are communicating. Pathos can be positive or negative, but we need to consciously decide what emotion we are eliciting in others through our communication and that can guide what we say and how we say it. Personally I am a fan of inspiring leadership, which means that when we connect people to their emotions, it's better to activate positive emotional states versus negative ones.

Case Study

Marcus is a highly regarded executive within a very profitable insurance company. He has held his position for 3 years and produced excellent ROI for the business and brought in many clients with very high life-time value to the business. Despite Marcus's tangible achievements within his role, some of his direct reports have complained to HR that he can lack emotion and compassion and come across as quite cold, making them feel far less motivated and productive as a result. When confronted with the thoughts of his team Marcus was surprised as he had not noticed any negative feelings from his team nor had he ever perceived himself as closed-off or unapproachable. Marcus admitted that he can often become curt or dismissive when under pressure, which is common due to the nature of his job, which can then result in him focusing more on what he is doing in order to achieve his targets and neglecting how his team is tracking. In order to cultivate Emotional Presence, Marcus started focusing on asking simple questions of his team members as a daily practice. From the basics (How are you? How is it going?) to the more targeted (Is there anything I can help with? How are you feeling about the prospects of expanding the client relationship?). He found that after a few weeks his team seemed more comfortable with him, and he asked them to let him know if he seemed distant or unapproachable, because he was aware that sometimes he seemed distant when he was really just trying to focus. That authentic expression of a desire to improve made his team much happier and more comfortable, and as time went on he developed more positive rapport across the group.

Tips and Exercises for Emotional Presence

"It is very important to understand that emotional intelligence is not the opposite of intelligence, it is not the triumph of heart over head – it is the unique intersection of both"
– David Caruso

Some simple steps Marcus could take to improve his emotional intelligence and relationships with his team include;

Be deliberate with every conversation
When Marcus assigns a new task, for example, he should go beyond the basic "Here are the details for your next design client," and reiterate why he truly values someone's work: "You did an incredible job designing that website last week. We have a new client who seems pretty choosy, and since your work is so detail-oriented, I think you're the only one for the job." Or, as Marcus starts giving people more challenging work, clearly acknowledge what he's doing and why: "You really did a fantastic job with the presentation during the team meeting last week, so I think you can handle a monthly client presentation with some of our big accounts." The more Marcus recognizes his employees' specific contributions to the team, the more irreplaceable they will feel.

Show them they are needed from others too

This is not to say that Marcus should never hesitate to reward his employees for a job well done, of course. But, it is beneficial to remember that feedback from others can pack a little more punch- and therefore Marcus should show his team that they are not only appreciated by him but also by clients, co-workers and fellow executives.

Champion them

Marcus needs to be more aware of what each person does best within his team and assign tasks accordingly. By doing this, it will help Marcus to convey a message to employees and co-workers that he entirely believes in their capabilities.

Acknowledge them as individuals

To truly make individual employees feel valued, it's fine for Marcus to single them out and reward them according to their accomplishments—and with something that the rest of the team won't necessarily get. Marcus could also pinpoint an employee to attend a conference on his behalf. Simple gestures go a long way: If Marcus sees an employee who has done something exceptional during the week, he can pull such aside and let her leave work an hour or two early on a Friday afternoon.

Exercise: Ask a Feeling Question

Sometimes in order to connect to someone's emotions we have to ask questions that get them thinking - and feeling!

Try some of these questions with your direct reports as an Emotional Presence experiment:

 a.How do you want to feel within the next (day, month, year) about your work at this company? I want to help you get there.

 b.What does success look and feel like for you?

 c.What motivates you to feel really excited about a project?

CHAPTER 4 – Charismatic Presence

"The essential difference with Builders is that they've found something to do that matters to them and are therefore so passionately engaged, they rise above the personality baggage that would otherwise hold them down. Whatever they are doing has so much meaning to them that the cause itself provides charisma and they plug into it as if it was an electrical current." --Jerry Porras

What is Charismatic Presence?

Charismatic presence is a person's aptitude at positively impacting those around them just by being in their company. It includes the ability to be confident within a group environment; having the presence to command an audience's full attention.

Charismatic Presence in Action

Charismatic Presence requires us to be aware that others view us as a role model and the degree to which we understand how our behavior impacts those around us. This is a crucial part in leading as a greater understanding of how one's own behaviors are perceived empowers a leader to have increased control on the impact and outcomes of their behaviors. A person that possesses Charismatic Presence is often described as having a magnetic personality; a person that exudes confidence and positivity and people genuinely want to not only be around, but listen to and follow. That Charismatic Presence can come from natural magnetism, or from our passion for what we are doing that radiates outward and engages others to want to be part of it.

When you have Charismatic Presence you are able to convey your thoughts and ideas to people in a way that gets them to feel the same purposeful commitment you feel. People will instinctively follow a person that is sure of where they are headed, they also tend to buy into your ideas whether they realize it or not. You may not always have a plan or direction, just take that first step and radiate a sense of clarity and precision and people will automatically look up to you, humans tend to always look for a leader, someone to guide them, prove to be that someone and they will run to you.

This particular skill could come in handy in times of distress, those moments when people hesitate to make a decision because they are not sure of the outcome or if it is a good idea, moments when all that is required is a single step, a show of single-minded direction will put you on that pedestal. Humans fear the unknown, a display of sheer fearlessness and boldness would attract them to you, very few people possess this trait and the few who do are regarded with awe.

Brian Hall was an author, professor, organizational consultant and researcher on human values in organizations. He wrote over 40 books including a seminal book called Values Shift, and was a truly knowledgeable expert on the concept of "presence". In Brian's research on values across cultures, he found that one of the core values across the globe (that is sometimes hard for us to articulate) is the value of Presence. Brian Hall and his research partner Benjamin Tonna defined Presence on the personal and organizational levels as:

Presence

➔*Personal Value: Spending quality time with another person so that he or she is able to ponder the depths of being with awareness and clarity. This comes from inner self-knowledge, which is so contagious it compels the other person to achieve the same state.*

➔*Corporate Value: Spending quality time with other persons that comes from inner self-knowledge, which is so compelling that teams, persons, or clients understand themselves with more clarity. They are energized into a quality exchange that leads to higher and more effective levels of creativity, respect, and complex problem solving.*

It is this type of presence that underscores Charismatic Presence. Those people with Charismatic Presence elicit the best in others through just being themselves. They have a depth of understanding of who they are that enables others to know their own value and worth. They bring out excellence and positivity through that quality of being.

In developing Charismatic Presence, you need to be good at telling stories. Stories are relatable and real. It brings life to the scenario or the business principle you are trying to convey. A great storyteller is very good at using examples, illustrations, facial gestures, body language and the right vocal inflections to pass across key points of the story. Your narrations can be delivered with a great sense of passion, moral conviction, engagement and purpose. As an effective storyteller, you may ask questions and engage your listeners to see how they feel and what they understand from what you are saying so far. The art of storytelling gets your staff and listeners to not just do what you are saying because you told them to, but because you have got them to believe in it.

In order to tell a good story you may need some practice. Some fun elements of telling a good story include vivid description, an inherent conflict, intriguing characters, and a punchy ending. For example, instead of saying "the woman went to the store" describe it - "Angrily Sheree drove 10 miles an hour on the freeway to get to her least favorite store, the Stop n Save." If you are the character you should describe something of yourself that's important to the story: "When I was a teenager I could not stop wearing my favorite black hoodie, which did not endear me to my teachers who were forever asking me to take my hood down and show my face. This was my first time realizing I needed Executive Presence, even though I didn't know it then."

Case Study: Charismatic Presence

Sophia has been working for the same company in the same role for the last 5 years, however the company has recently done some restructuring which has resulted in the refinement of job descriptions of many employees. Sophia has previously only had three direct reports which she had built very close relationships with over the last 5 years and established a very strong sense of mutual respect. Through the restructuring, Sophia now has 7 direct reports and dotted lines to another 4.

Sophia is excited about her greater responsibilities, however is concerned with how she is going to be able to gain the respect of such a large team with whom she has not had the chance to build relationships with over the last few years. Sophia would not describe herself as an overly shy or timid person, however she is not confident in her ability to instantly gain the respect of her subordinates and be able to inspire results. She has met some of the people she is now responsible for individually and is concerned that they may naturally project greater presence or authority which will detract from her efforts in leading the team.

Sophia decided to tell a story to her new team about herself as a college athlete as an illustration of what it can take to win as a team, and how much she values teamwork and collaboration. That story had two effects - one was to give the team a metaphor to guide their vision of the future, and two it had a powerful impact on Sophia's level of confidence by structuring the narrative in her favor.

Tips for Greater Charismatic Presence

Some aspects of leadership in relation to Charismatic Presence to take note of are:

Rigour
We need to exhibit rigor as leaders. We should always bring to the forefront the tenacity that comes with success. As leaders with Charismatic Presence, we have to acknowledge that we are not experts on every business process, product line or service, however we have to be rigorous practitioners of what we preach. The art of leadership involves our skills of management and the tools of decision making and analysis. We need to "walk the talk" by demonstrating that we have thought through our work, and that we understand the elements that other people are responsible for, even if we are not directly doing that work ourselves. People listen to us when we demonstrate that we do what we say we will do, that we understand our shared context, and when we let them know that we are listening.

Curiosity

As leaders with Charismatic Presence, it is a time to keep learning, unlearning and relearning. We need to actively seek out knowledge that makes us fresh. The process of doing this can be challenging to our preconceived ideas. It can also update our reasoning and trigger creativity and innovation. Nothing engages others like our own sense of curiosity. It encourages others to develop a growth mindset.

Confidence

Actually, nobody is purely confident that they know everything and can handle every situation that could arise at all times. As leaders with Charismatic Presence, we know that no matter what happens there are solutions to implement or lessons to be gained, and that when bad things happen that ultimately we will prevail. That sense of commitment to a positive outcome makes others feel confident with you.

Resilience

When we opt to take every situation we encounter as a change to learn, grow, change or develop, it gives us the capacity to weather many storms in life and work. That attitude of resilience provides a strong foundation for influencing others to be more effective and fulfilled. It also gives us the inner strength to engage others to solve problems, face challenges or changes with their own best efforts.

Exercise: Storytelling Research

Step One: Find three good storytellers and watch them tell an engaging story. This can be as simple as going online and listening to a few TED talks or podcasts to find stories that really work.

Step Two: Think of a story you want to tell, and practice on a friend, colleague, partner or child! Kids are great at giving blunt and honest feedback to make your story better. They'll tell you to amp up your voice, act out the words, and make it entertaining.

Step Three: Try it out for real. Tell a story to someone at work that illustrates a core concept.

About the Author

Karlin Sloan is the founder and CEO of Sloan Group International. Karlin has committed herself to finding out what makes great leaders tick, and to supporting leaders to be the change they wish to see in the world. As a corporate citizen she is an advocate for triple-bottom-line reporting, for creating sustainable ways of working and living, and for creating positive organizational communities that work together for the greater good. For more about Karlin Sloan visit https://www.linkedin.com/in/karlinsloan/.

About Sloan Group International

Sloan Group International is a premier provider of leadership development programs for Fortune 500 companies and emerging entrepreneurial organizations. We have a proven track record of expertise in large-scale leadership development and executive coaching programs. Our programs have resulted in achievement of individual goals as well as significant business results. We believe each individual is responsible for being a role model – for "being the change" they wish to see in the world.

Helping organizations to thrive through Inspiring Leadership is our specialty. Our approach offers a blend of consulting, coaching and mentoring for both individuals and teams, and is backed up with a range of industry leading assessments and various practical, usable tools. We use cutting-edge research in neuroscience, positive psychology, leadership, organizational development and systems thinking to shape our offering.
Like our approach, our programs are unique and customized to address your specific needs. SGI is known for our ability to manage and staff large scale executive coaching programs worldwide, and to provide unique, customized leadership programs which inspire and motivate leaders to connect to their greatest talents and perform with flexibility, ease, and heightened self-awareness.

Our core programs create the foundation for Effective, Enduring, and Fulfilled Leadership, and receive rave reviews from our clients who see measurable, sustainable results for their organizations.

We regularly get over 500% measurable ROI for our programs for major multinational firms through large-scale executive development and leadership programs which have resulted in achievement of individual goals and business results, from retaining top talent to gaining productivity.

Join Us...

SGI's best-in-class Executive Presence & Influence Program (EPI) goes beyond traditional presentation skills coaching to offer a full-spectrum approach to building capabilities and competence in four key areas of Executive Presence: Somatic, Mental, Emotional, and Charismatic. Our workshops and integration coaching provide attendees a high dose of self-awareness through our proprietary self-assessment, video playback, one-on-one and group coaching, skill building and practical application of techniques and models. The result of our EPI program is to give you the confidence to embody all facets of your individual Executive Presence, which will enable you to drive impact, be influential, and build trust both inside and outside your organization.

We invite you to join us in developing your Executive Presence & Influence skills at www.sloangroupinternational.com.

www.ingramcontent.com/pod-product-compliance
Lightning Source LLC
Chambersburg PA
CBHW061105210326
41597CB00021B/3989